SUPERCARS

FERRARI

Ryan Smith

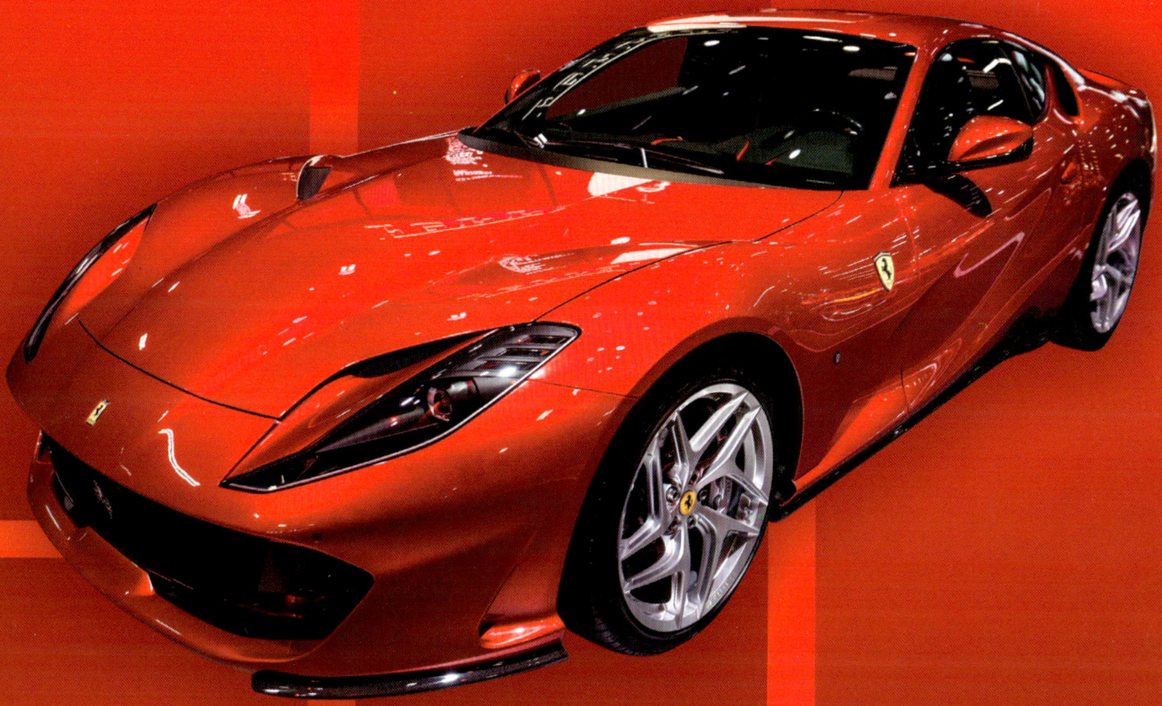

AV2
www.av2books.com

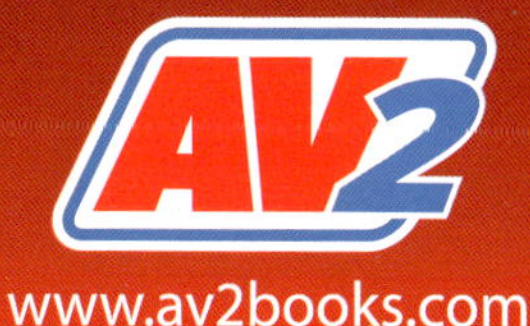

Step 1
Go to **www.av2books.com**

Step 2
Enter this unique code
BLFPJ4GCR

Step 3
Explore your interactive eBook!

AV2 is optimized for use on any device

Your interactive eBook comes with...

Contents
Browse a live contents page to easily navigate through resources

Audio
Listen to sections of the book read aloud

Videos
Watch informative video clips

Weblinks
Gain additional information for research

Try This!
Complete activities and hands-on experiments

Key Words
Study vocabulary, and complete a matching word activity

Quizzes
Test your knowledge

Slideshows
View images and captions

... and much, much more!

SUPERCARS

FERRARI

CONTENTS

FERI
Ferrari

RARI

FERRARI SUPERCARS

Supercars are made to go fast, but so are sports cars. So what makes supercars so special? Is it that they pack even more **horsepower** than sports cars? Is it that supercars cost hundreds of thousands of dollars? Or is it that so few supercars are made each year? For a car to be a supercar, it has to be rarer, more powerful, and more expensive than a sports car.

For more than 70 years, Ferrari has made rare car **models**. Each model is faster, sleeker, and more **luxurious** than the last. Today, Ferrari is one of the most recognizable supercar brands to speed down the road.

Ferrari set a company **sales record** in 2019 when it sold more than **10,000** cars.

In 2018, a **1963 Ferrari 250 GTO** was sold for **$70 million**.

ENZO FERRARI

"Everyone dreams of driving a Ferrari, it was my intent from the start." -Enzo Ferrari

Enzo Ferrari started out as a race car driver. He founded his own race team in 1929. It was called Scuderia Ferrari. His team worked for a car maker called Alfa Romeo. Scuderia Ferrari raced for Alfa Romeo until 1937.

Enzo started the Ferrari car company in 1947. His first car was the Ferrari 125S. It came in first place in the Rome **Grand Prix** in 1947.

Ferrari's first race car driver, Franco Cortese, drove the 125S to victory at the 1947 Rome Grand Prix.

MAP OF ITALY

Enzo Ferrari saw his first motor car race in Bologna, Italy, when he was 10 years old.

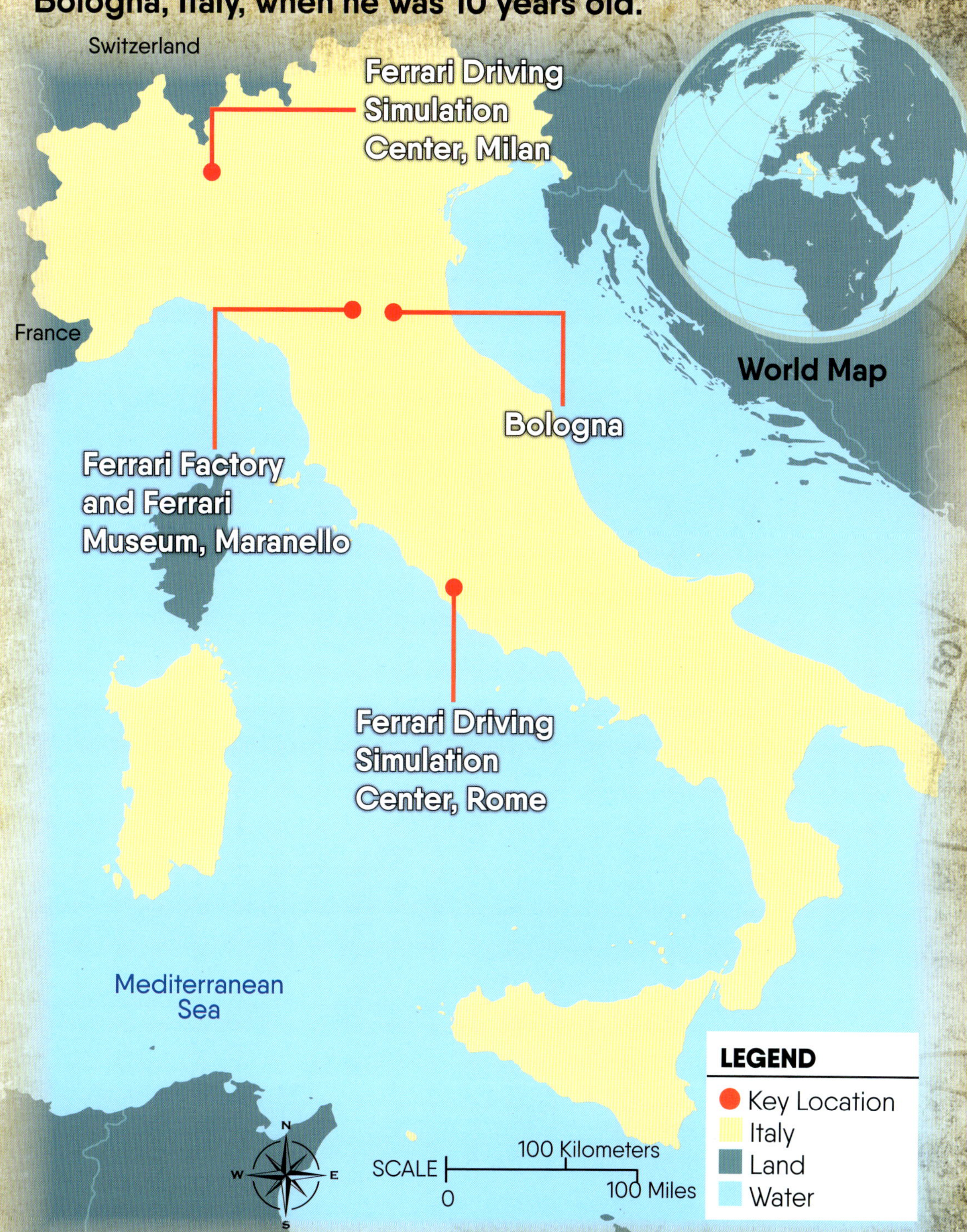

THE PRANCING HORSE

Francesco was a pilot who became an Italian hero in **World War I**. He had a prancing horse painted on his plane. Enzo met Francesco Baracca's parents in 1923. Francesco's mother told Enzo to use the horse for his car company's logo. She said it would bring him good luck.

Francesco was Italy's most successful World War I airman.

FERRARI LOGO

The colors of the Italian flag run across the top of the logo.

The background is canary yellow. The same color is found on the Coat of Arms of Enzo's hometown of Modena, Italy.

The S and F at the bottom of the logo stand for Scuderia Ferrari.

FERRARI THROUGH HISTORY

Ferrari started out as Enzo's dream. Today, it is known around the world as an icon of style, luxury, and speed.

Ferrari builds its first race car, the 125S.

1947

1951

1988

Enzo Ferrari dies at age 90.

Ferrari wins its first **Formula 1 (F1)** Championship Grand Prix.

2002

The first Ferrari Store opens in Maranello, Italy. It sells Ferrari merchandise such as clothing and jewelry.

2010

The Ferrari World theme park opens in Abu Dhabi, United Arab Emirates.

2020

Ferrari launches the SF1000 race car for the 2020 F1 racing season.

FAMOUS FERRARIS

Ferrari is famous both on and off the racetrack. Some Ferraris have found even more fame by appearing in movies and famous collections. In 2019, the racing rivalry between Ferrari and Ford made its way to the big screen in *Ford v Ferrari*.

Six different Ferrari models appeared in *Ford v Ferrari*.

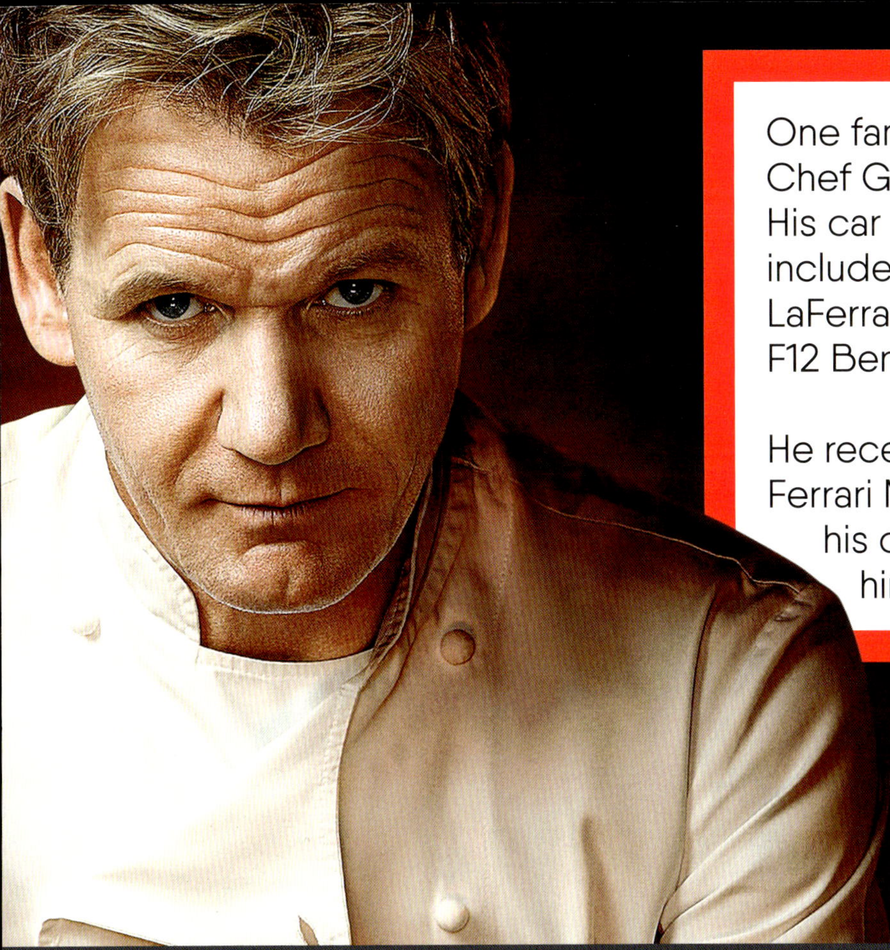

One famous collector is Chef Gordon Ramsey. His car collection includes the Ferrari LaFerrari and Ferrari F12 Berlinetta.

He recently added the Ferrari Monza SP2 to his collection. It cost him $2 million.

Ferrari LaFerrari

Ferrari F12 Berlinetta

Ferrari Monza SP2

AT THE RACES

Since its beginning, Ferrari has focused on winning races. Today, Ferrari takes part in both F1 and **Grand Touring (GT)** racing.

Ferrari's F1 racing team is still called Scuderia Ferrari. Ferrari will race in its 1,000th F1 race in 2020. Ferrari also organizes its own race series called the Ferrari Challenge. These races are for Ferrari customers who want to do more than just drive their Ferraris on the street.

Ferrari's Fernando Alonso won the Bahrain F1 Grand Prix in 2010.

In 2019, the Ferrari 250 GTO was recognized as a work of art by the Italian government.

Ferrari's **quickest pit stop** took **1.9 seconds.**

A **Ferrari F1** car will drive **27,960** miles (45,000 kilometers) in a single season.

F1 pit crews will do thousands of practice pit stops in a season.

Ferrari driver Sebastian Vettel won the Singapore F1 Grand Prix in 2019.

HOW IT'S MADE

Ferraris are built in a factory in Maranello, Italy. Almost every part of a Ferrari is put together by hand. The factory has two robots named Romeo and Juliet. They help build the engines. Each car moves around the factory on a **lift**. The lift rotates the car so that each part can be easily attached.

The Ferrari assembly line covers an area of more than 226,040 square feet (21,000 square meters).

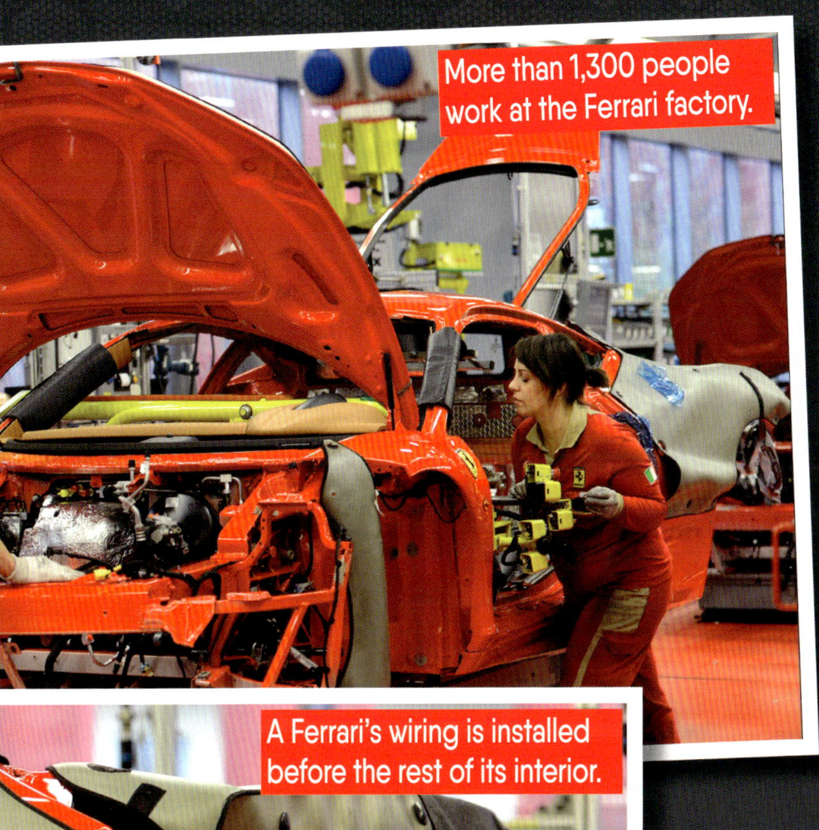

More than 1,300 people work at the Ferrari factory.

It takes **three months** to **build a Ferrari**.

Less than **8,400** Ferraris **are made** each year.

A Ferrari's wiring is installed before the rest of its interior.

147 Ferrari engines are hand-built every day.

TODAY'S LINEUP

Ferrari still captures Enzo's passion for racing. Today's Ferrari models each offer something different. The Ferrari GTC4 Lusso seats four people. The Ferrari SF90 Stradale is the company's first **hybrid** vehicle.

Here are some of the Ferraris on the road today.

Ferrari Roma

Engine: **V8**

Maximum Horsepower: **620**

0–60 mph (0–100 km/h): **3.4 seconds**

Starting Price: **$225,000**

Ferrari F8 Tributo

Engine: **V8 Turbo**

Maximum Horsepower: **720**

0–60 mph (0–100 km/h): **2.9 seconds**

Starting Price: **$279,450**

Ferrari GTC4 Lusso

Engine: **V12**

Maximum Horsepower: **690**

0–60 mph (0–100 km/h): **3.4 seconds**

Starting Price: **$298,900**

Ferrari 488 Pista

Engine: **V8**

Maximum Horsepower: **720**

0–60 mph (0–100 km/h): **2.8 seconds**

Starting Price: **$331,000**

Ferrari 812 Superfast

Engine: **V12**

Maximum Horsepower: **800**

0–60 mph (0–100 km/h): **2.9 seconds**

Starting Price: **$338,000**

Ferrari SF90 Stradale

Engine: **V8 and three electric motors**

Maximum Horsepower: **780**

0–60 mph (0–100 km/h): **2.5 seconds**

Starting Price: **$625,000**

TOMORROW'S FERRARI

Enzo Ferrari once said, "The best Ferrari that has ever been built is the next one." Ferrari uses its **concept cars** to find ways to make its cars faster, more powerful, and more fuel-efficient.

The Ferrari Monza SP1 and the Ferrari Monza SP2 are part of Ferrari's Icona concept series. They combine designs from the past with the performance of the future. These Ferraris feature Virtual Wind Shields. Instead of a glass windshield, the shape of the car forces air over and away from the driver.

The interior of the Monza SP1 is inspired by Ferrari's race cars.

The Monza SP1 can go from 0 to 60 mph (0-100km/h) in 2.9 seconds.

The Monza SP1 seats just one person. The Monza SP2 seats two.

The look of the Monza SP1 is inspired by past Ferrari designs.

FERRARI QUIZ

1 What makes a car a supercar?

2 In what year did Enzo start his race team?

3 What was the first car Ferrari made?

4 Which country's flag colors are on the top of the Ferrari logo?

5 How much money did Gordon Ramsey pay for his Ferrari Monza SP2?

6 How fast was Ferrari's quickest pit stop?

7 What are the names of the two robots that help assemble Ferrari engines?

8 How long does it take to build a Ferrari?

9 Which model is Ferrari's first hybrid vehicle?

10 Do the Ferrari Monza SP1 and the Ferrari Monza SP2 have Virtual Wind Shields?

ANSWERS

1 More powerful, more expensive, and rarer than a sports car **2** 1929 **3** The Ferrari 125S **4** Italy **5** $2 million **6** 1.9 seconds **7** Romeo and Juliet **8** Three months **9** The Ferrari SF Stradale **10** Yes

KEY WORDS

concept cars: a car built to show off new technologies and designs

Formula 1 (F1): the highest level of single-seat car racing

Grand Prix: a series of high-level races

Grand Touring (GT): a race car that seats two people

horsepower: the equivalent power that is produced by one horse pulling

hybrid: a car that is powered by both a gas engine and an electric motor

lift: a device used to raise and lower a vehicle while it is being worked on

luxurious: something that is pleasing and comfortable

models: the different car designs made by a company

World War I: a war that was fought mainly in Europe from 1914 to 1918

INDEX

Get the best of both worlds.

AV2 bridges the gap between print and digital.

The expandable resources toolbar enables quick access to content including **videos**, **audio**, **activities**, **weblinks**, **slideshows**, **quizzes**, and **key words**.

Animated videos make static images come alive.

Resource icons on each page help readers to further **explore key concepts**.

Published by AV2
14 Penn Plaza, 9th Floor
New York, NY 10122
Website: www.av2books.com

Library of Congress Cataloging-in-Publication Data

Names: Smith, Ryan, author.
Title: Ferrari / Ryan Smith.
Description: New York, NY : AV2, [2021] | Series: Supercars | Audience: Ages 7-12. | Audience: Grades 4-6.
Identifiers: LCCN 2020014474 (print) | LCCN 2020014475 (ebook) | ISBN 9781791125783 (library binding) | ISBN 9781791125790 (paperback) | ISBN 9781791125806 | ISBN 9781791125813
Subjects: LCSH: Ferrari automobile--Juvenile literature.
Classification: LCC TL215.F47 S65 2021 (print) | LCC TL215.F47 (ebook) | DDC 629.222--dc23
LC record available at https://lccn.loc.gov/2020014474
LC ebook record available at https://lccn.loc.gov/2020014475

Printed in Guangzhou, China
1 2 3 4 5 6 7 8 9 0 24 23 22 21 20

062020
101119

Art Director: Terry Paulhus Project Coordinator: Ryan Smith

Every reasonable effort has been made to trace ownership and to obtain permission to reprint copyright material. The publisher would be pleased to have any errors or omissions brought to its attention so that they may be corrected in subsequent printings.

The publisher acknowledges Alamy, Getty Images, Shutterstock, and Wikimedia Commons as its primary image suppliers for this title.